PARAMEDICS

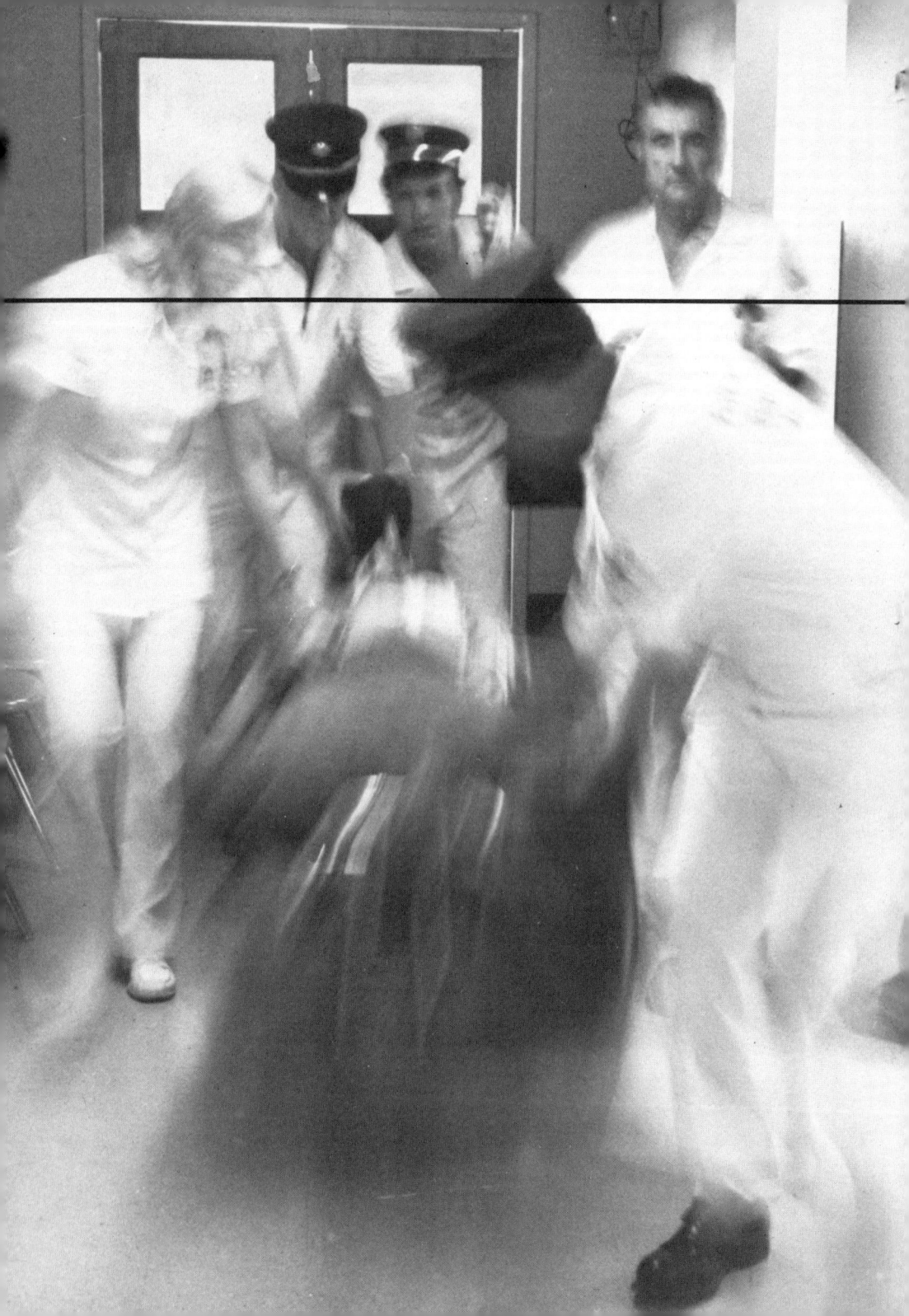

PARAMEDICS

By Walter Oleksy

Illustrated with Photographs

Julian Messner
New York

Copyright © 1983 by Walter Oleksy

All rights reserved including the right of
reproduction in whole or in part in any form.
Published by Julian Messner
A Division of Simon & Schuster, Inc.
Simon & Schuster Building,
1230 Avenue of the Americas,
New York, New York 10020.
Julian Messner and colophon are trademarks of
Simon & Schuster, Inc.

10 9 8 7 6 5 4 3 2

Manufactured in the United States of America

Design by Prairie Graphics

Library of Congress Cataloging in Publication Data.

Oleksy, Walter G.
   Paramedics.

   Bibliography: p.
   Includes index.
   Summary: Discusses the origins of paramedics in the United States and the life-saving emergency work that they do.
   1. Emergency medical technicians—Juvenile literature. 2. Emergency medical services—Juvenile literature. 3. Emergency medical technicians—United States—Juvenile literature. 4. Emergency medical services—United States—Juvenile literature.
   [1. Allied health personnel. 2. Occupations]
   I. Title.
RA645.5.038   1983   616'.025   83-13388
ISBN 0-671-44274-0

Acknowledgments

With gratitude to Captain Phil Burns, Paramedic Gary Swanson, and the Evanston, Illinois, Fire Department Mobile Intensive Care Unit. Special thanks to James O. Page, editor of *jems*, the *Journal of Emergency Medical Services*.

Messner Books by Walter Oleksy
Paramedics
Nature Gone Wild
Treasures of the Land
It's Women's Work, Too!

PHOTO CREDITS

ACT Foundation, title page
City of Miami Fire Dept., photo by Carl Mertens, pp. 15, 16
Columbus, Ohio, Division of Fire, p. 11
Evanston (Illinois) Hospital, p. 29
Ingalls Memorial Hospital (Harvey, Illinois), pp. 38, 56
Los Angeles County Fire Dept., p. 30
Medical Services, Inc., p. 21
National Broadcasting Co., p. 40
Walter Oleksy, pp. 23, 32
Phoenix (Arizona) Fire Dept., p. 47
Physio-Control Corp., photo by Bob Peterson, pp. 8, 44–45
Salt Lake City (Utah) Fire Dept., pp. 20, 50–51
Thurston County (Washington) Fire Dept. District #3, p. 49
Zee Medical Products Co., pp. 19, 28, 33, 53

CONTENTS

1 •	Emergency!	9
2 •	Before Paramedics	12
3 •	Why "Paramedics?"	17
4 •	A Typical Paramedic Unit	22
5 •	Mutual Aid Emergency System	27
6 •	Paramedics In Action	31
7 •	Problems Facing Paramedics	39
8 •	Careers in Paramedics	52
9 •	How You Can Help	57
	For Further Information	59
	Suggested Further Readings	61
	Index	62

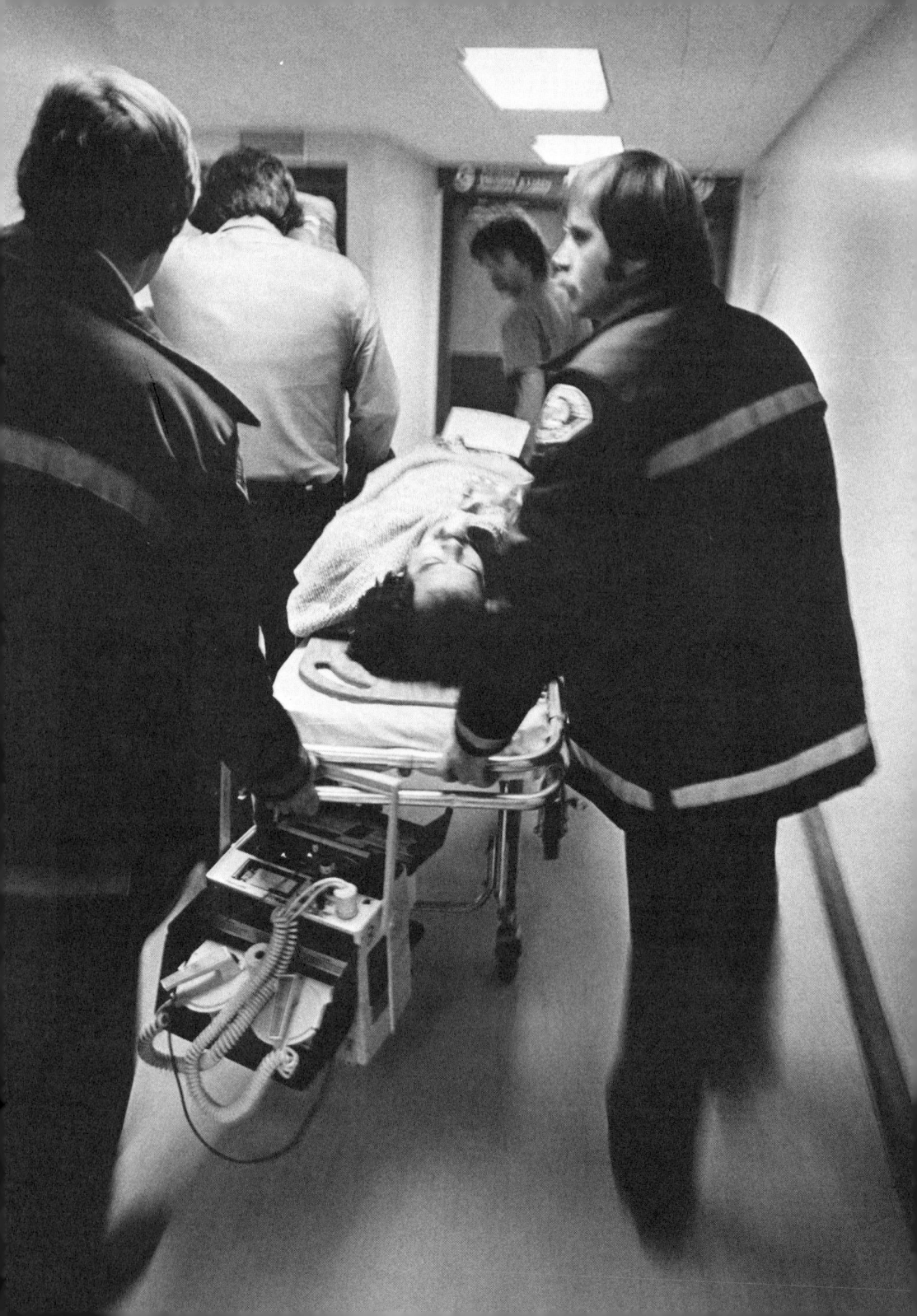

CHAPTER 1

EMERGENCY!

A SPARK FROM a lighted firecracker flew onto a pile of fireworks. They exploded close to 15-year-old Tim Rogers' face. Tim's mother heard the explosion and raced to the phone to call the fire department when she saw her son fall.

The department's paramedic team was dispatched immediately to the Rogers home, and within minutes Tim was being given emergency treatment. The paramedics radioed the nearest hospital to report on the kind of burns Tim had. They also radioed information on Tim's vital signs—his blood pressure, breathing, heartbeat, and pulse. The paramedics applied special burn dressings and gave Tim oxygen. Then Tim was sped by ambulance to a waiting Air National Guard helicopter for transfer to a special burn unit at nearby Evanston Hospital in Illinois.

The Evanston Fire Department's Mobile Intensive Care Unit (MICU) waited at the heliport for Tim, who was quickly transferred to the paramedic ambulance for the drive to the hospital. Emergency room doctors were ready with everything Tim needed.

Tim had suffered burns on his face, chest, hands, and arms. But he recovered fully in due time, thanks to the fast emergency action by paramedics and hospital burn specialists.

Every minute of every hour all across the country, paramedics are called to help people suffering burns like Tim, or heart attacks, or drug overdoses, or injuries from automobile crashes, or the many other accidents and illnesses that occur.

No one can count how many lives have been saved by the paramedics since 1967 when the first unit in the United States began their jobs.

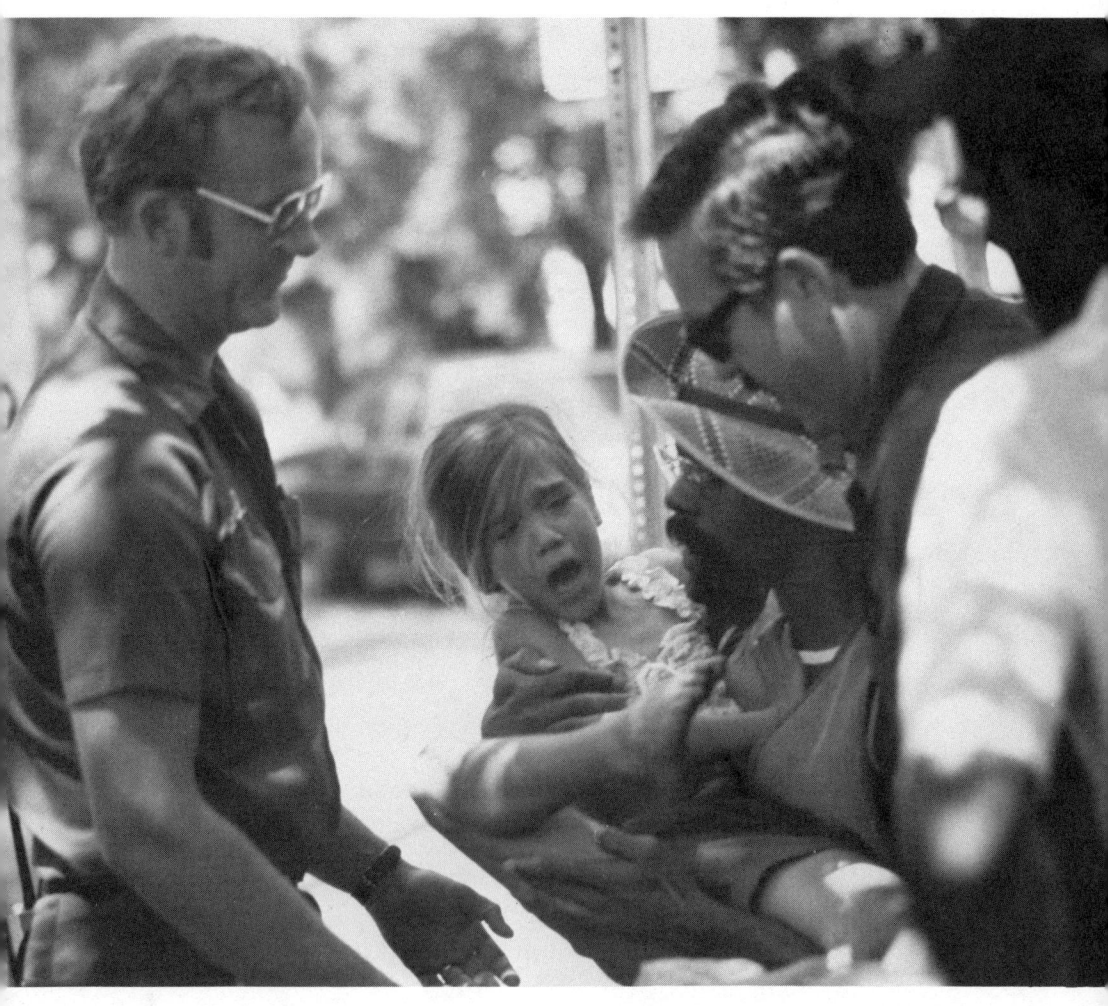

Paramedics arrive and will soon help this little girl's pain—she has stepped barefoot into hot tar.

CHAPTER 2
BEFORE PARAMEDICS

EMERGENCY MEDICAL and ambulance service to the public has been available for many years. But ambulances, either privately operated or sent from a hospital, had only simple first aid equipment like tourniquets to stop bleeding, bandages, and splints. Sometimes hospital ambulances had doctors riding with them, but most often ambulances carried only the driver and a helper, trained to treat only the simplest medical emergencies.

In the 1950s, the Russians began sending out ambulance crews consisting of a doctor, nurse, and a special physician's assistant. In 1961, doctors in West Germany and in France began going along on ambulance calls.

But a heart doctor in Belfast, Ireland, Dr. Frank Pantridge, had a better idea. Instead of wasting precious time taking a patient to the hospital—even under a doctor's care—Dr. Pantridge thought it made better sense to send the hospital out to the patient. He devised the first mobile unit for the care of heart patients, the closest thing yet to a "hospital on wheels." Like the earlier Russian teams, a doctor, nurse, and medical student rode in an ambulance with the most modern medical equipment to wherever someone needed immediate care. Dr. Pantridge's unit began to be called a "Flying Squad." They gave medication and oxygen, and if the victim's heart had stopped beating, they administered electric shock to start it beating again.

Doctors at St. Vincent's Hospital in New York City soon started a similar mobile heart unit in 1966. Not long after, a "Heartmobile" was used in Columbus, Ohio, with firemen going along as part of the emergency medical rescue team.

Emergency medical care for heart attack patients improved, but other emergencies were still not getting the care they needed. Doctors and nurses were

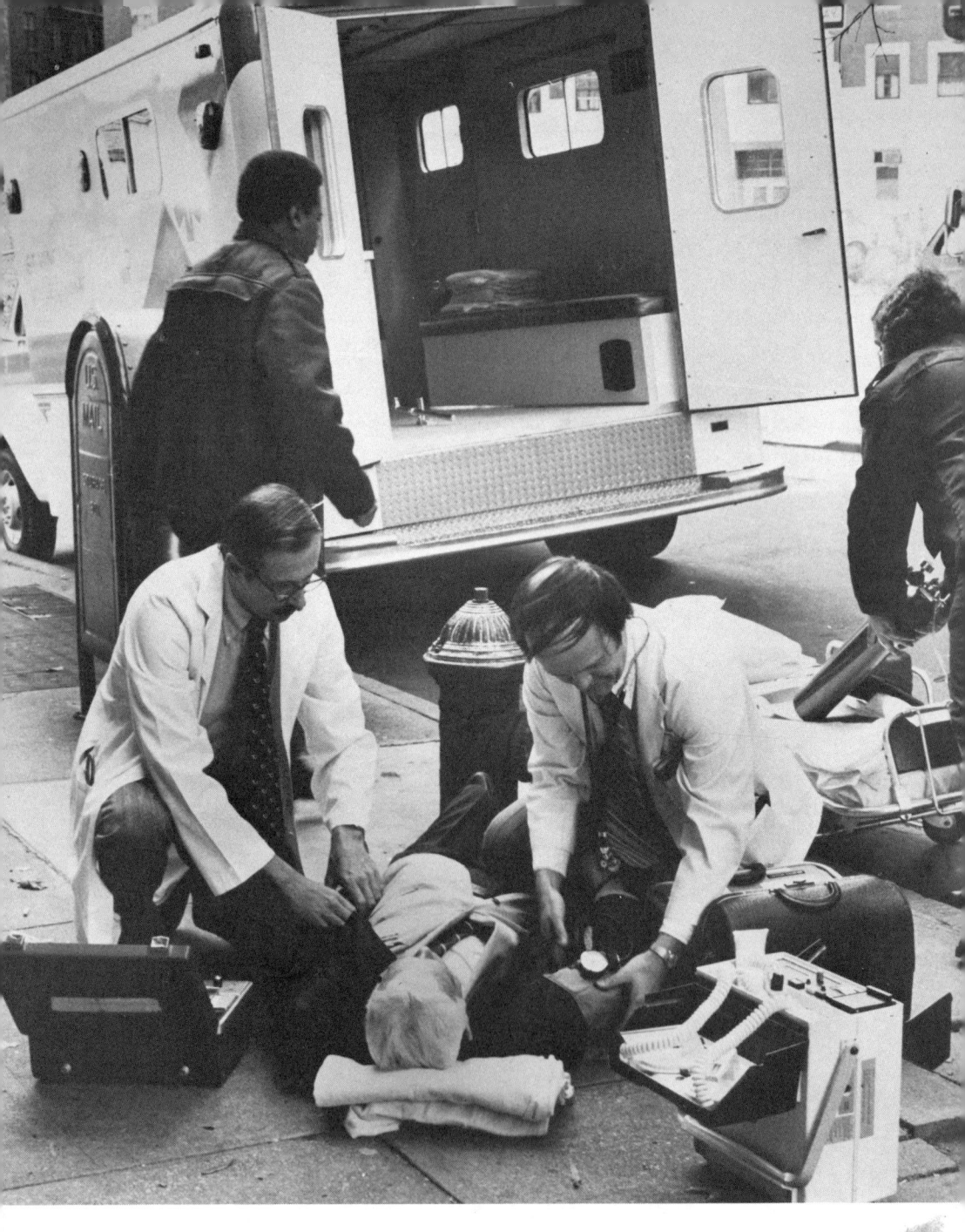

Mobile coronary care unit of St. Vincent's Hospital, New York City, brings immediate care to a patient stricken on the street.

in too short supply to leave the hospitals and ride ambulances. And drivers' helpers still did not know enough to handle serious emergencies.

One thing that was needed was better communication between the ambulance crews and the doctors waiting for the patient in the hospital. Advances in radio and telephone communications made this communication possible. Trained medical technicians could now send information from the scene of an emergency directly to the doctors in hospitals.

The radio-telephone system was developed by Dr. Eugene Nagel in the late 1960s. It was also his idea to

Dr. Eugene Nagel is hooked up to his first radiotelephone system (in milk crate).

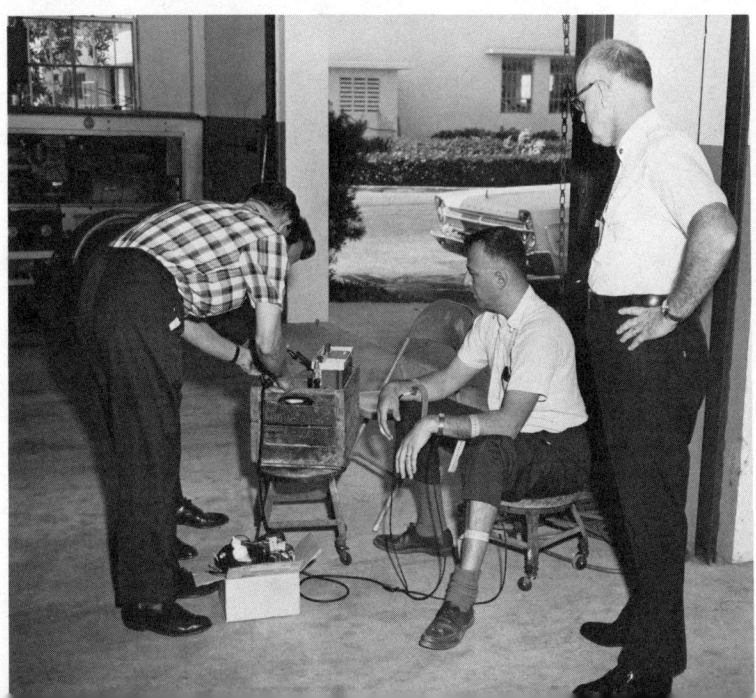

train firemen as emergency medical technicians, because firemen are already trained in first aid and the handling of emergencies.

Dr. Nagel is called the "Father of Paramedics," and this was the real beginning of today's paramedics.

Dr. Nagel (far right, in surgical cap and gown) instructs America's first paramedic trainees at University of Miami School of Medicine.

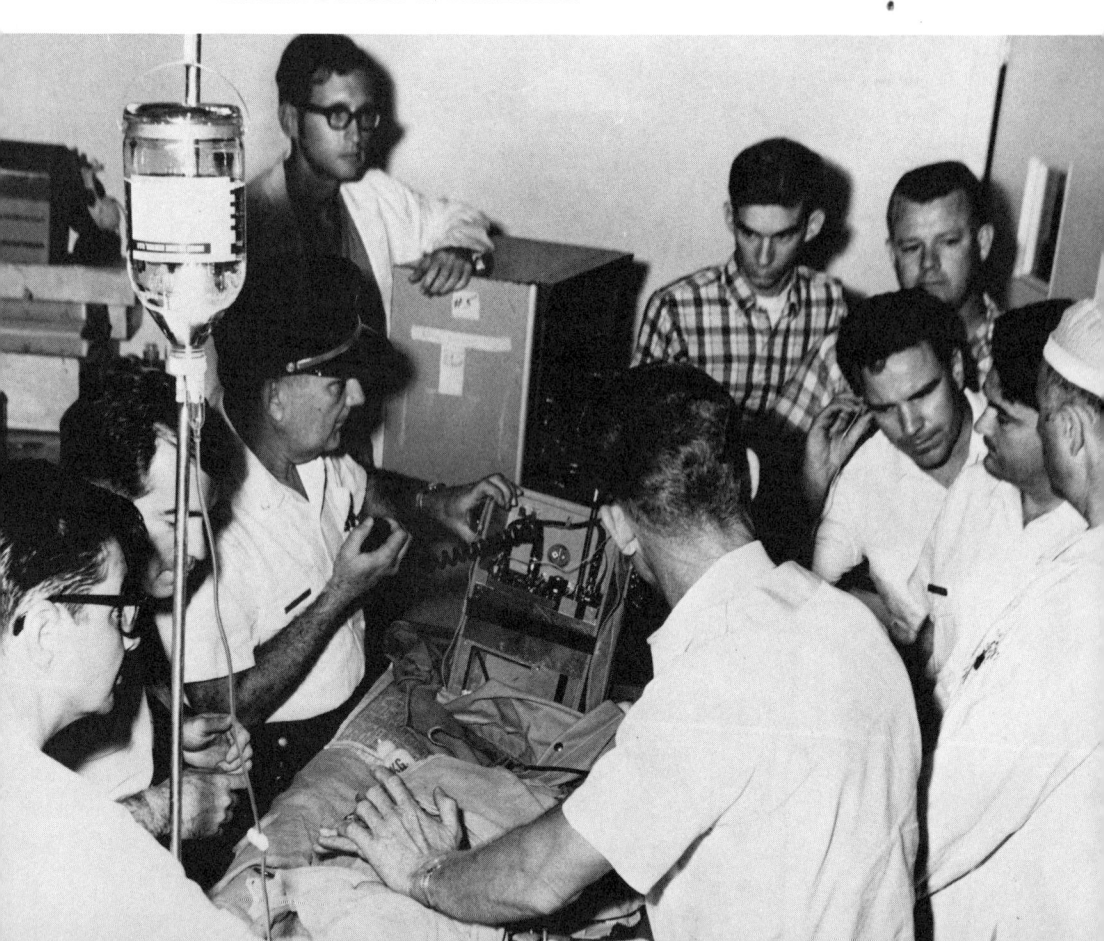

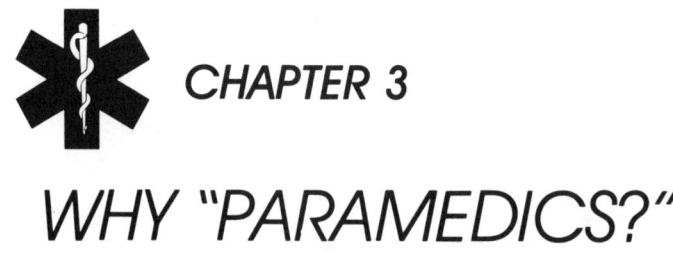

CHAPTER 3

WHY "PARAMEDICS?"

No one knows exactly where the word "paramedic" comes from. The word may have military origins, referring to medically trained paratroopers.

In the first years paramedics still went by various names, such as "EMTs"—emergency medical technicians—"Cardiac Rescue Technicians" and "Physician's Trained Mobile Intensive Care Paramedics."

In 1966, Congress passed the Highway Safety Act

Paramedics—highly trained experts, here wearing special reflective jackets for safety at night.

Electrocardiogram machine.

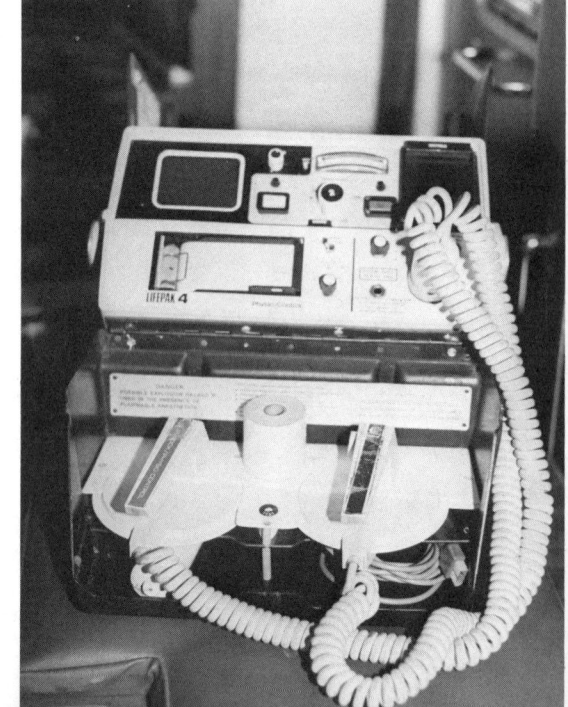

providing money to the states so they could buy ambulances and train medical crews to ride in them. The United States Department of Transportation taught firemen, policemen, and ambulance crews first aid, emergency childbirth care, heart massage, and mouth-to-mouth resuscitation. After completing 81 hours of instruction, graduates were certified emergency medical technicians.

Before long, most states required that anyone transporting sick or injured people had to take the training and become a certified EMT.

An EMT has the basic training needed for an ambulance technician. He or she can take blood pressure; administer CPR (cardio-pulmonary resuscitation); do a body survey for broken bones, cuts, and sprains; apply splints and bandages; and perform other basic first aid treatment on a patient. An EMT gives *basic* life support to the victim.

But this is not always enough. Very often someone is needed to handle more advanced life support functions. And so a training program was set up to teach more advanced care—paramedic training.

A paramedic is allowed to administer life-supporting drugs, and run electrocardiograms that produce graphs of the patients' heart functions and are transmitted electronically to the hospital. The paramedic can also operate a machine that delivers an electric shock to restart a heart that has stopped.

A paramedic is applying electrodes on chest of victim of smoke inhalation in order to monitor his heart activity by electrocardiogram while another paramedic is readying an oxygen mask. The paramedic at the far left is in touch with doctors at a hospital to relay information back and forth.

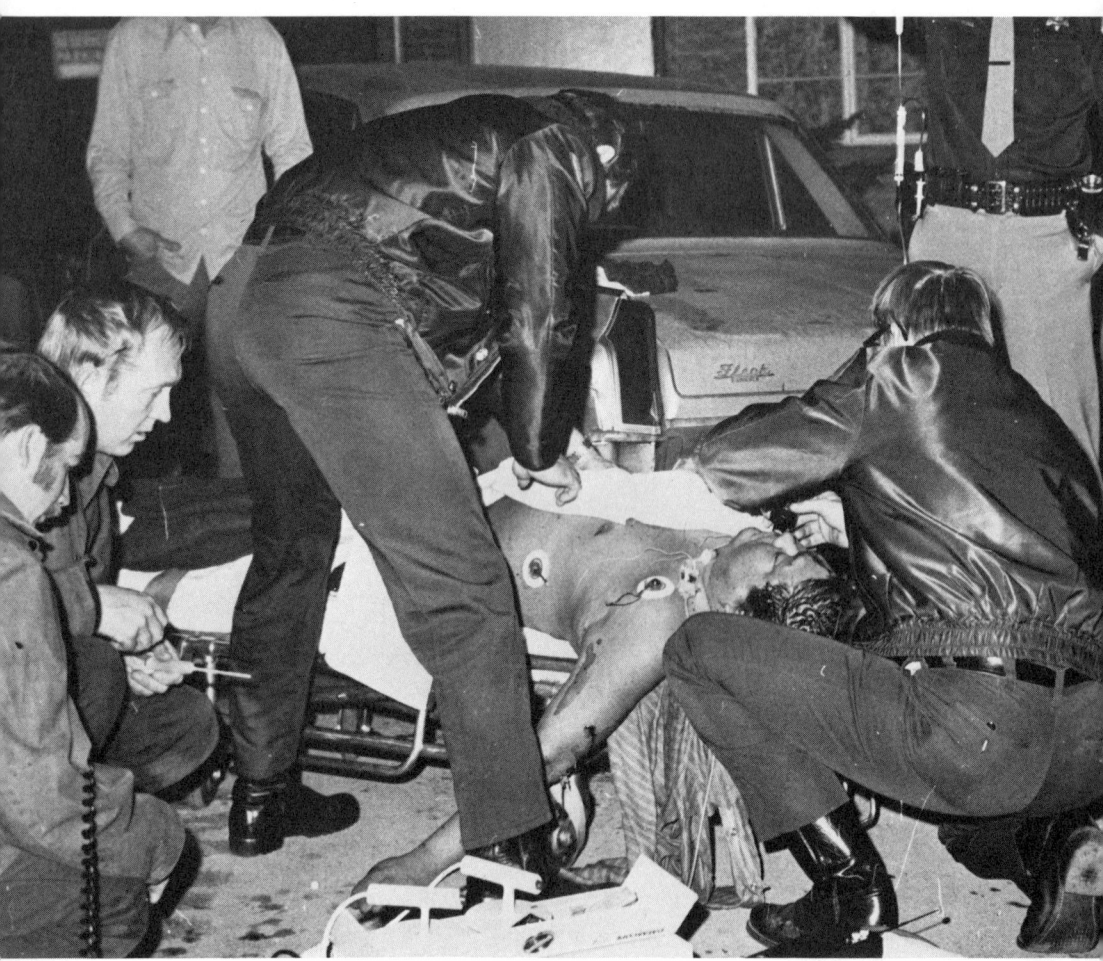

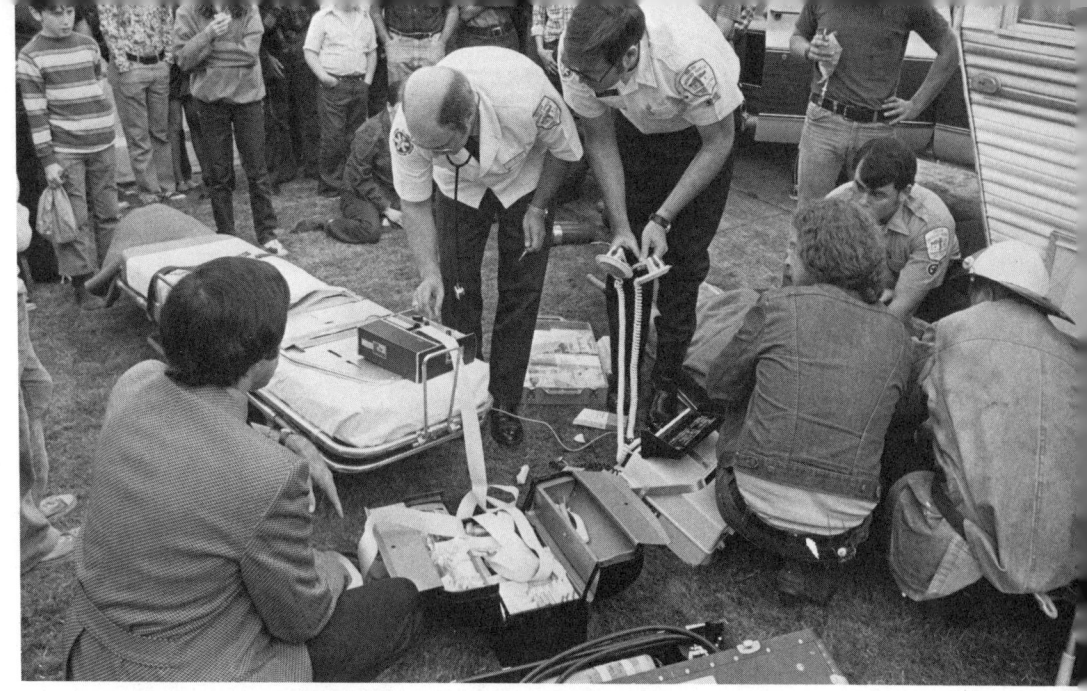

Studying a patient's heart activity before using the defibrillator (in hands of paramedic on right).

The process is called "defibrillation." And a paramedic can give medication as instructed by a doctor over the radio-telephone. Paramedics can start intravenous medication—drugs that are administered by a constant dripping from a bag or bottle through a tube and needle inserted into a vein. Paramedics can perform a tracheotomy, a surgical incision of the trachea or windpipe to allow air to get into the lungs when there is something blocking the air supply.

Paramedics are lifesavers!

CHAPTER 4

A TYPICAL PARAMEDIC UNIT

EVANSTON, ILLINOIS, a suburb just north of Chicago, with a population of about 80,000, has a paramedic system that is typical of units throughout the nation. The system is called the "Mobile Intensive Care Unit of the Evanston Fire Department" and has 56 EMTs and 38 registered paramedics.

Each fire department ambulance carries one EMT and one paramedic. In some towns and cities, depending on the size and training of staff, two

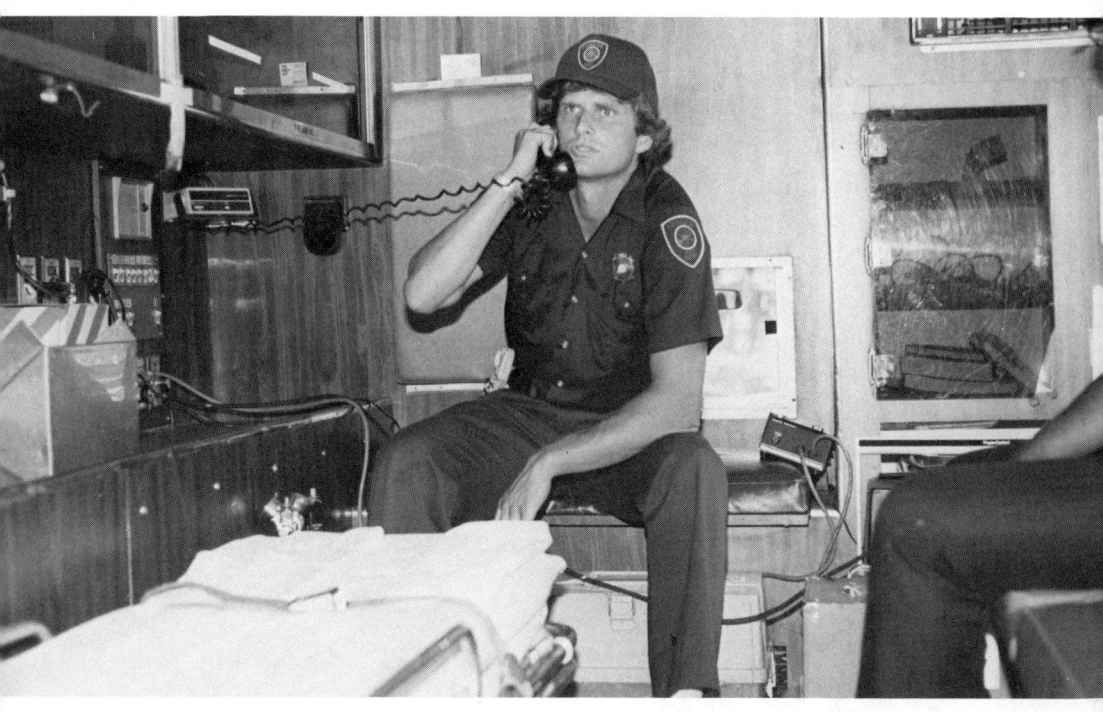

This specially-equipped ambulance allows paramedic Gary Swanson of Evanston to give advanced life support to a patient being rushed to hospital.

paramedics or two paramedics and an EMT make up the ambulance crew.

Evanston's paramedic unit has three ambulances with advanced life support equipment and one with basic life support equipment for taking victims to the hospital. A fire engine company also responds to every call.

In Evanston, all paramedics are firemen first. After working as firefighters, they can apply to take instruction to become EMTs or paramedics.

Trainees take seven months of instruction at St. Francis Hospital in Evanston, either on days off from work or on time off to attend classes. The paramedic interns must pass a final practical test and then a written test. Then they must take statewide practical and written tests which are often much more difficult.

EMTs and paramedics also attend training programs at St. Francis Hospital to keep up their basic skills. They take 40 hours of instruction in new techniques and refresher courses.

In some cities, such as Chicago, paramedics only do medical work and do not fight fires. In other cities, paramedics work some days as paramedics, other days as firefighters, to help prevent a problem called "paramedic burnout." When a paramedic rides an ambulance constantly, he or she can get disturbed after a while at seeing people in bad

Paramedics work hard.

emergency situations. It helps to let paramedics do other work part of the time.

Paramedics also take part in instructing the public. They demonstrate first aid, CPR, and other emergency medical techniques to school children, senior citizens, Boy and Girl Scouts, and other groups of people.

Calls for paramedic help are varied and seemingly endless. Paramedics answer calls in which kids have been bitten by animals, fallen from trees or bicycles, or badly injured in car crashes. One boy was electrocuted during a lightning storm. Paramedics were able to save his life.

In a recent blizzard, Evanston paramedics had to reach a heart attack victim. Some of the snow-covered streets were impassable, so the unit went by snowmobile. They administered drugs at the scene, tied the victim to a toboggan, and got her to an ambulance that sped her to the hospital.

CHAPTER 5

MUTUAL AID EMERGENCY SYSTEM

EVANSTON'S PARAMEDIC UNIT is also part of the Chicago suburban M.A.B.A. (Mutual Aid Box Alarm) system. This system is for local communities to coordinate medical service during major emergencies. Most smaller cities and towns around the country band together in the same way to meet disasters.

In a major emergency or disaster such as a tornado, a fire producing many injuries, a train or plane wreck, each unit has its own emergency job to do. Paramedic units may be called in from distant locations to help at the emergency scene or to stand in for units that have been moved from *their* home bases to answer the emergency call.

If an emergency occurs in Evanston, for instance, 16 ambulances can be drawn to the area from other locations in the M.A.B.A. system. If more are needed, they are called in from Chicago. Ambulances are dispatched by an operator at the Central Dispatch Center. The operator also can call for boats or helicopters to help, if necessary.

Recently, there was an emergency at a large chemical company. Seventeen people were overcome by toxic fumes, and three of them went into cardiac arrest. Captain Phil Burns, in charge of the paramedic unit, declared a disaster for the city.

"We pulled out all the resources we have," Captain Burns says. "We used the mutual aid system. Ambulances came in from other suburbs and even our police squad cars were used as transporting vehicles to take victims to the hospitals. We had communication at the scene, en route to the hospitals, and at the hospitals." This spread the load and made the situation more manageable.

Sometimes Evanston paramedics work with the U.S. Coast Guard to help rescue swimmers or boaters on Lake Michigan. Weather changes fast on the lake and small boats may not be able to reach shore safely when storms build up suddenly. A boat overturns and people find themselves swimming for their lives, often in dangerously cold water, until a Coast Guard boat or helicopter can pluck them out. Paramedics are usually aboard the rescue boat or helicopter, or are waiting on shore to give emergency medical treatment for injuries, near-drowning, or shock.

Recently, the captain aboard a freighter on the lake suffered a heart attack. The Coast Guard airlifted him by helicopter and Evanston paramedics met them on shore to care for the captain as they sped him to the hospital.

On another call, paramedics helped rescue a man

A helicopter ambulance sets down on a golf course where paramedics stand by to rush the patient to a nearby hospital.

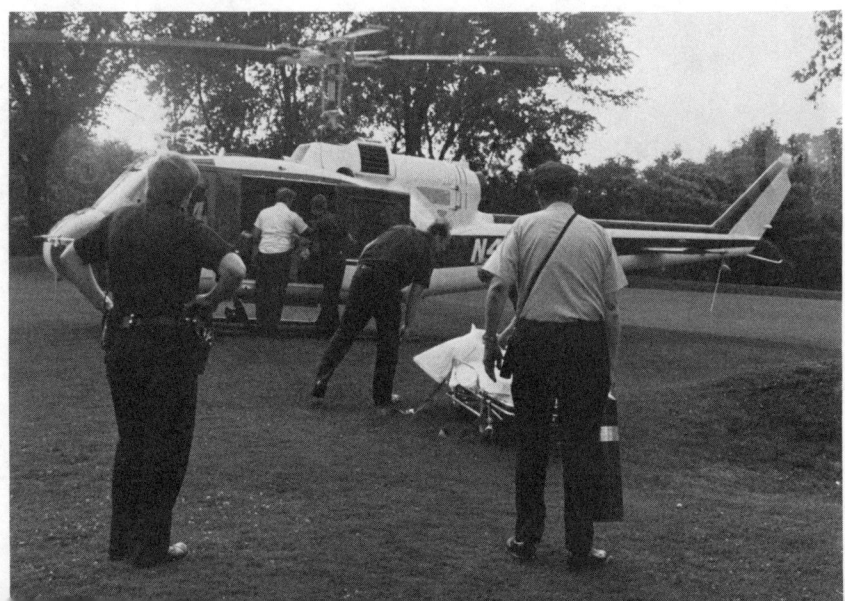

who had been injured while working 200 feet down in a sewer tunnel.

Some paramedics are called to help in emergencies outside the United States. After an earthquake in Guatemala in 1976, when paramedics from Burbank, California, were flown to help victims, a rescue organization was formed and called "M.E.D.I.C.S. International." "M.E.D.I.C.S." stands for Medical Emergency Disaster Intensive Care Specialists. Members are paramedics, doctors, and nurses, who volunteer to help anywhere in the world.

Paramedics work in all kinds of places—here, on a ranch to help the victim of a fall.

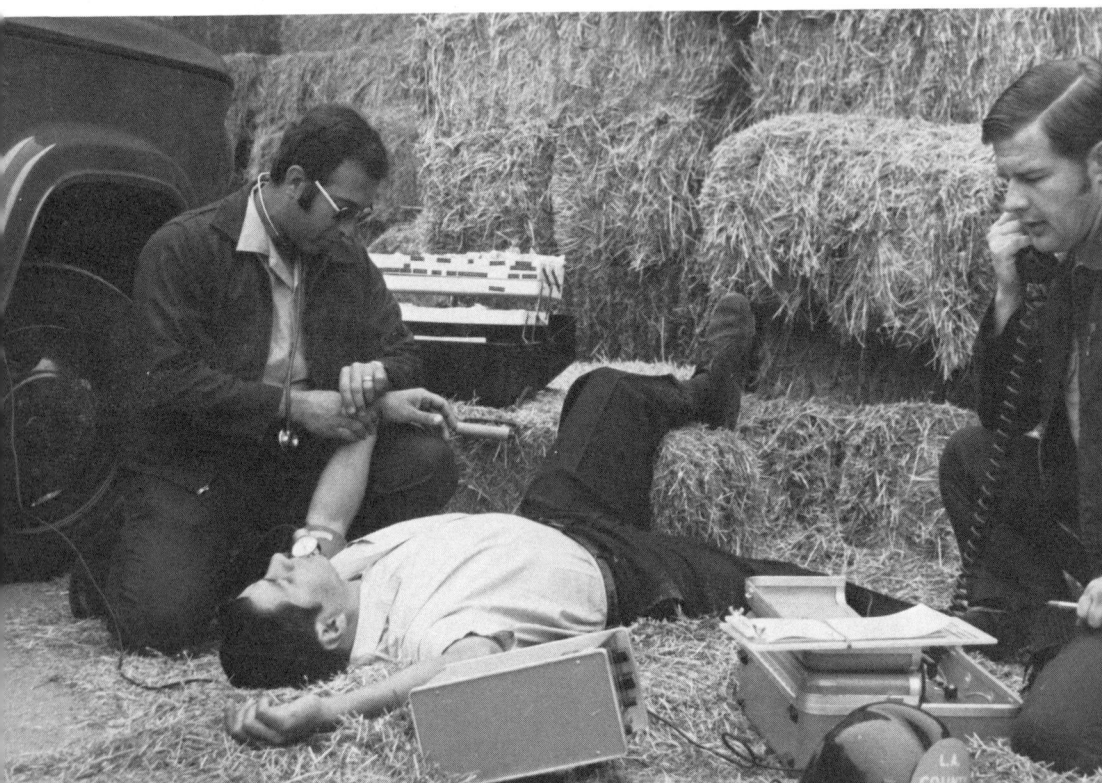

CHAPTER 6

PARAMEDICS IN ACTION

WHILE WORKING A SHIFT, a paramedic eats and sleeps at the fire station, the usual base for most units, and takes turns shopping for groceries and cooking meals and cleaning up.

At the start of a shift, the paramedic checks to be certain the ambulance or paramedic truck is fully equipped and everything is in good working order. The trucks and equipment have to be in perfect condition and ready to pass inspection.

Whoever reaches a victim first, whether firefighter

Supplies must be kept in good order in ambulance....

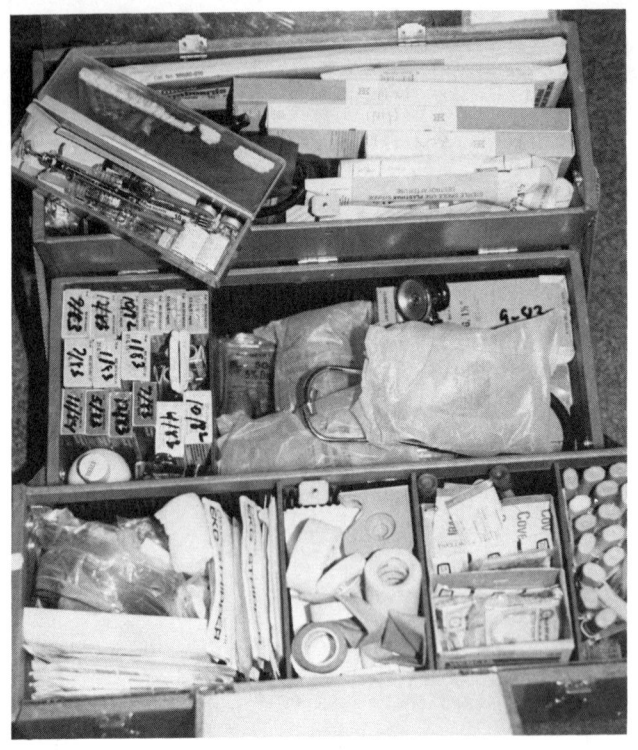

. . . .and in the soft trauma pack, which holds blanket, resuscitator, stethoscope, burn sheet, scissors, bandages, and other essentials.

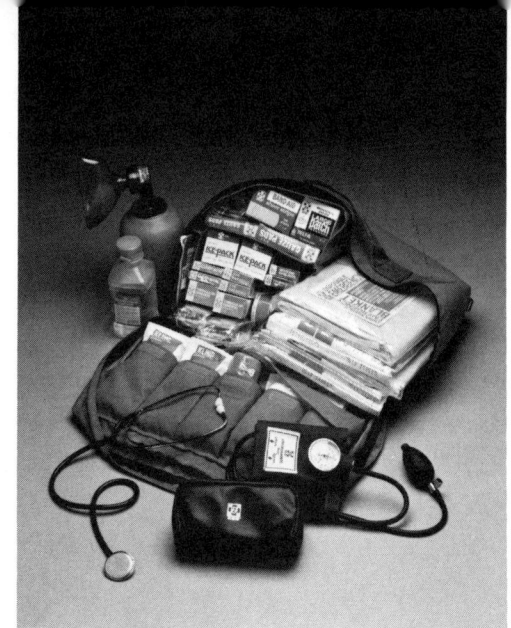

You can see why—it would be a waste of precious time and effort to have to come back down a ladder, for instance, to find something that was missing from the pack.

or paramedic, checks if the person is breathing and takes his or her pulse. If he or she is not breathing, CPR is begun. Next, first-aid treatment is given for any bleeding, broken bones, or burns. If a firefighter starts treatment, the paramedic takes over as soon as possible.

Patients may not need to be taken to a hospital—a paramedic can sometimes give enough care at the scene so they can be sent home. If a patient must be taken to the hospital, the paramedic alerts the hospital as to the ETA—estimated time of arrival—of the ambulance. Then paramedics take the victim to the hospital as fast as possible, continuing to tend to the patient on the way.

When there is need for medical help at the scene of an emergency, the central fire department dispatcher is contacted. The dispatcher alerts the fire station closest to the emergency.

When the emergency bell goes off, a fire station becomes a beehive of activity. At night, the lights go on automatically. "Squawk boxes"—loudspeakers—blare out brief information about the emergency: what it is, where it is, and who is to respond. Firefighters upstairs in their living quarters grab their gear and slide down the slippery pole to where the trucks and ambulance wait. Sirens screaming and red dome light flickering, they are off within minutes of a call.

Dispatching a call for help.

Once the patient is turned over to the hospital emergency room staff, the paramedic's job turns to doing paperwork. A report form has to be filled out on each run for various agencies or city departments. Then it's back to the fire station to wait for the next emergency. It might be something like this:

The loudspeaker at Evanston's west side fire station blares. An ambulance is needed. Someone has had a heart attack.

The four-man paramedic unit arrives at a house some blocks from the station only minutes after the call has come in. A policeman is already there, holding members of the family back so that the paramedics can get to the victim lying in the hallway at the foot of the stairs.

Each paramedic has his or her own job to do and does it swiftly and efficiently. One applies CPR (cardio-pulmonary resuscitation) to the unconscious patient. Another is in radio communication with a nurse at Evanston Hospital's emergency room. She relays advice to the paramedics from a doctor on duty.

The woman's pulse fades. One of the paramedics prepares a hypodermic needle while another tries to get the woman to breathe with an oxygen mask.

It is urgent to get the patient to the hospital. The paramedics radio the emergency room at Evanston Hospital to say they will be there in seven minutes.

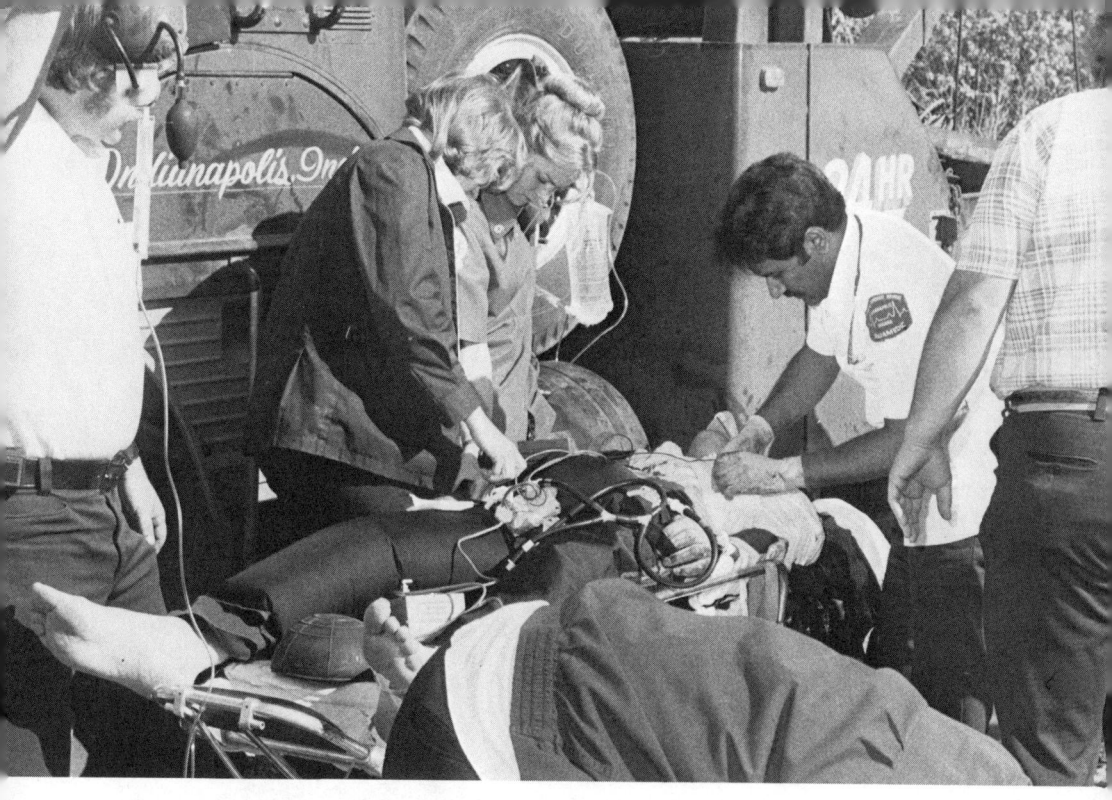

Every member of the team has his or her special job to do. Here one administers an IV, another cleans a wound, still another applies shock trousers, while others monitor heart activity.

The paramedics continue to help her with CPR and oxygen.

She is a very lucky woman. Emergency room physicians get her heart going properly again and her life is saved, thanks to their work and the fast team effort of the paramedics unit.

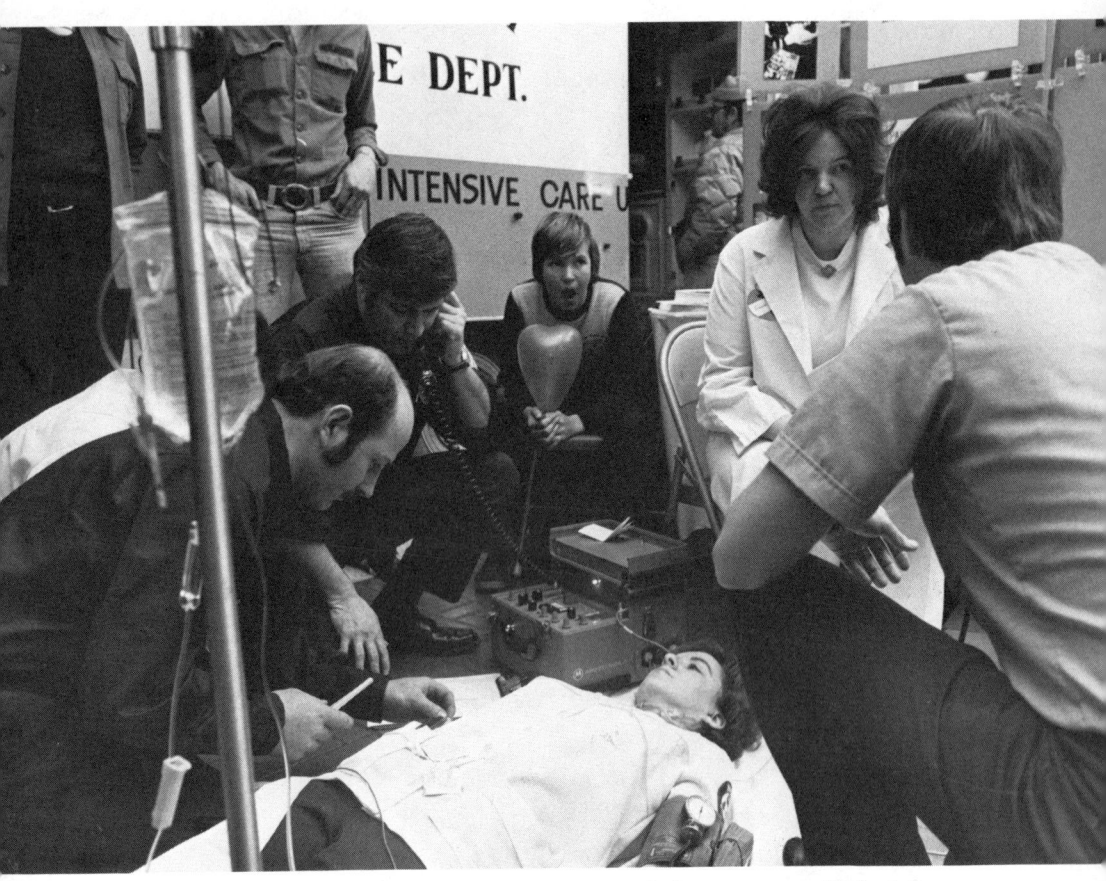

Public education is also part of the paramedic's job. Here, South Cook County (Illinois) paramedics demonstrate lifesaving techniques to passers-by in a shopping center.

CHAPTER 7

PROBLEMS FACING PARAMEDICS

With actors Randolph Mantooth and John Gage as paramedics acting out adventures drawn from real life paramedics cases, *Emergency!* became a hit TV series for NBC in the early 1970s and ran for several years. It is seen in reruns today in many parts of the country. The TV series brought the work of paramedics to the attention of the public and also of community leaders and influenced the formation of paramedic units in many parts of the country and around the world.

Randolph Mantooth (left) and Kevin Tighe portray paramedics in the TV series that brought the attention of millions of viewers to the work of the paramedics.

While the work of a paramedic can be exciting and rewarding, paramedics face many problems that come with such a high-pressure job.

Sometimes, strange as it may seem, paramedics are not as welcome as might be expected when they arrive at the scene of an emergency. In a high-crime neighborhood, paramedics may find their work downright dangerous. In Chicago a paramedic team refused to enter a housing project until police arrived to offer some protection against gangs of hostile teenagers.

Paramedics working in heavily populated neighborhoods may be called out constantly. They may have little or no time to relax, much less get some sleep. Going from one emergency to another with little time off in between can wear out a paramedic both physically and emotionally. For that reason, paramedics is considered young men's work. There are only a few women paramedics, although many EMTs are women. Even strong, healthy young men who are paramedics do not usually plan to work in the job long enough to retire in it. As one paramedic put it, "Who wants to carry people down two flights of stairs when you're 50 years old?"

Most communities with paramedic units are trying to get more ambulances and to hire more men and women as EMTs and paramedics to help relieve the heavy workload. But that costs money, and the hard economic times of the early 1980s have caused many communities to cut budgets. Starting or expanding paramedic units is one of the services hit by lack of money. Too often, ambulances can afford to carry only one paramedic and one or two EMTs. But EMTs can't do the work that trained paramedics do.

Getting this workman out of where he fell into sewer line is tough work.

A sad example of an understaffed emergency medical team happened not long ago in Chicago. Two EMTs, the entire crew of an ambulance, arrived at an emergency scene where a man had fallen with a heart attack. When the EMTs found they could not handle the situation without a paramedic, they called for a backup ambulance. The backup ambulance arrived only 12 minutes later—but that was 27 minutes after the original call for an ambulance had gone in. Paramedics on the second ambulance found no pulse on the patient when they arrived, but there was some heart activity. Desperately, the paramedics, aided by the EMTs, worked on the man for more than half an hour before they risked transporting him to the closest hospital. But it was too late. The man died.

"It hurts," says one paramedic. "It really hurts to come into a situation as a backup, way too late because you were not the first ambulance called, and find that maybe, if paramedics had been working the responding rig, maybe you could have saved a life.

"When you lose somebody, when they die, it stays with you. People are dying out there and I'm not sure all of them have to be DOAs (dead on arrival at a hospital). We don't have enough people on those ambulances. We don't have enough trained paramedics. And we don't have enough ambulances. It's a sad situation.

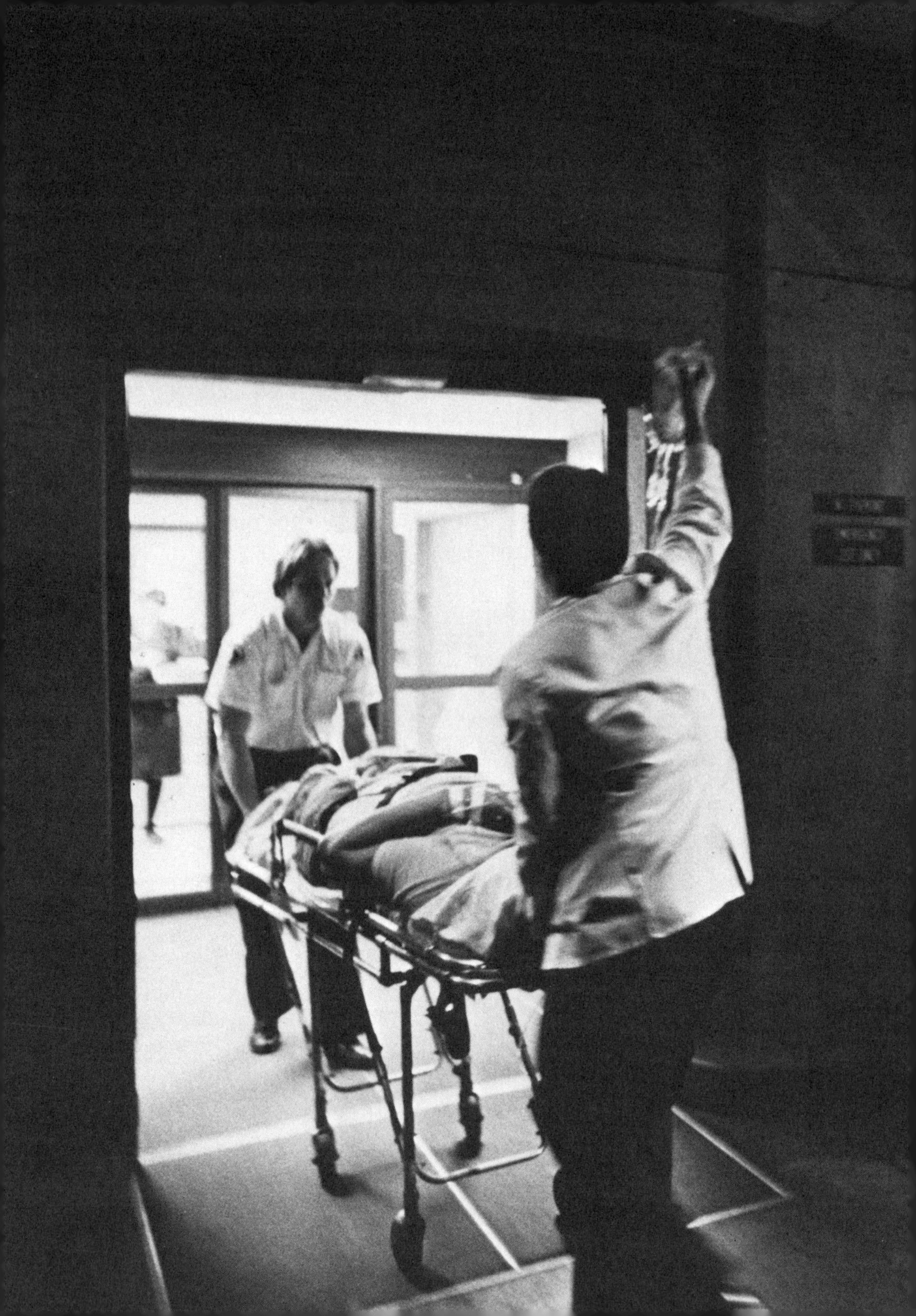

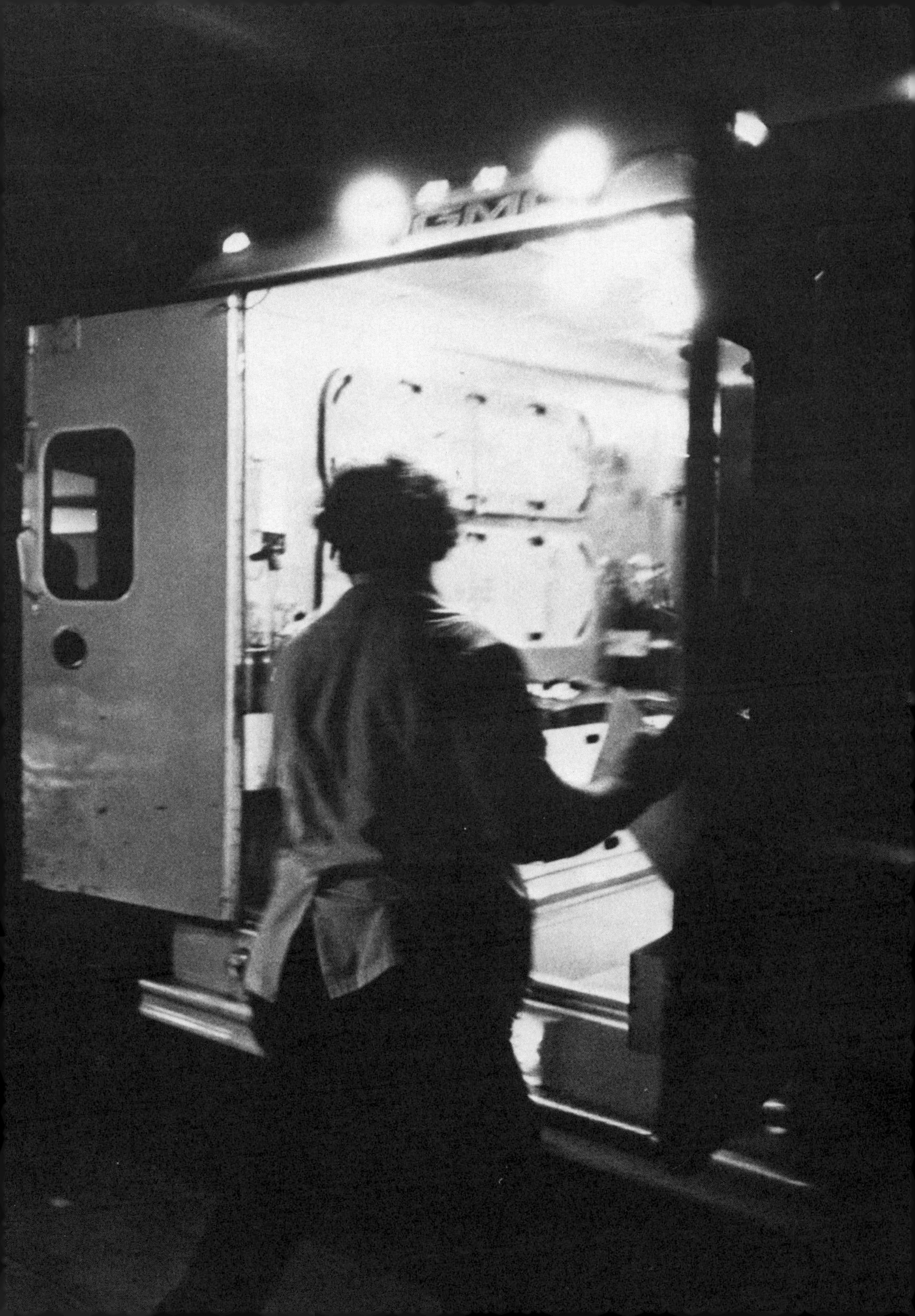

"I think it's interesting that a city can put four people on a garbage truck, but only two on an ambulance. Garbage can wait. A life can't."

It is no wonder, say some directors of paramedic units, that there is a serious paramedic burnout problem today. Many paramedics, overworked and disillusioned, are leaving to study nursing or respiratory therapy or other medical specialties. Or they are shifting to firefighters' jobs that may be less frustrating and which often have far better benefits and chances for promotion than the paramedics have. In many cities, firefighters can retire after 23 years of service at the age of 53. Paramedics can retire after 20 years, at age 55, but with only half the benefits.

Unequal workload is another serious problem affecting paramedics in many cities. A paramedic ambulance stationed in a relatively quiet neighborhood may only be sent out on five calls in a 24-hour shift. But a unit in a densely populated and high-crime neighborhood may make as many as 32 runs in the same period, permitting paramedics little or no rest or sleep in 24 hours.

Sometimes equipment gets overused and there is not enough time to inspect it before going out on another run. Or supplies dwindle before they can be replaced. Sending an ambulance out that is not fully operational can frustrate and defeat the paramedic aboard. Even minor equipment breakdowns can pre-

It takes a lot of work and equipment to save lives.

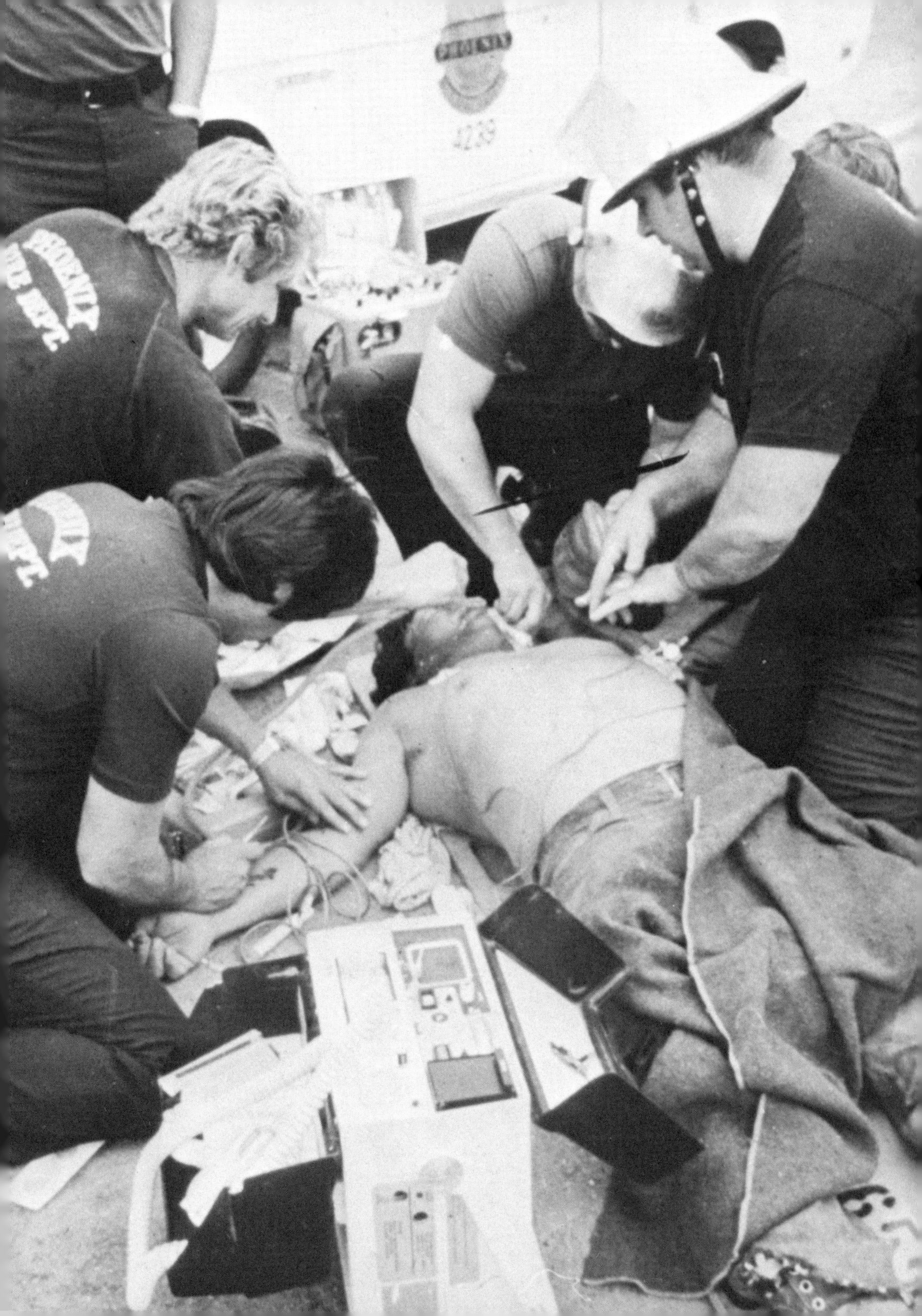
PHOENIX
4239

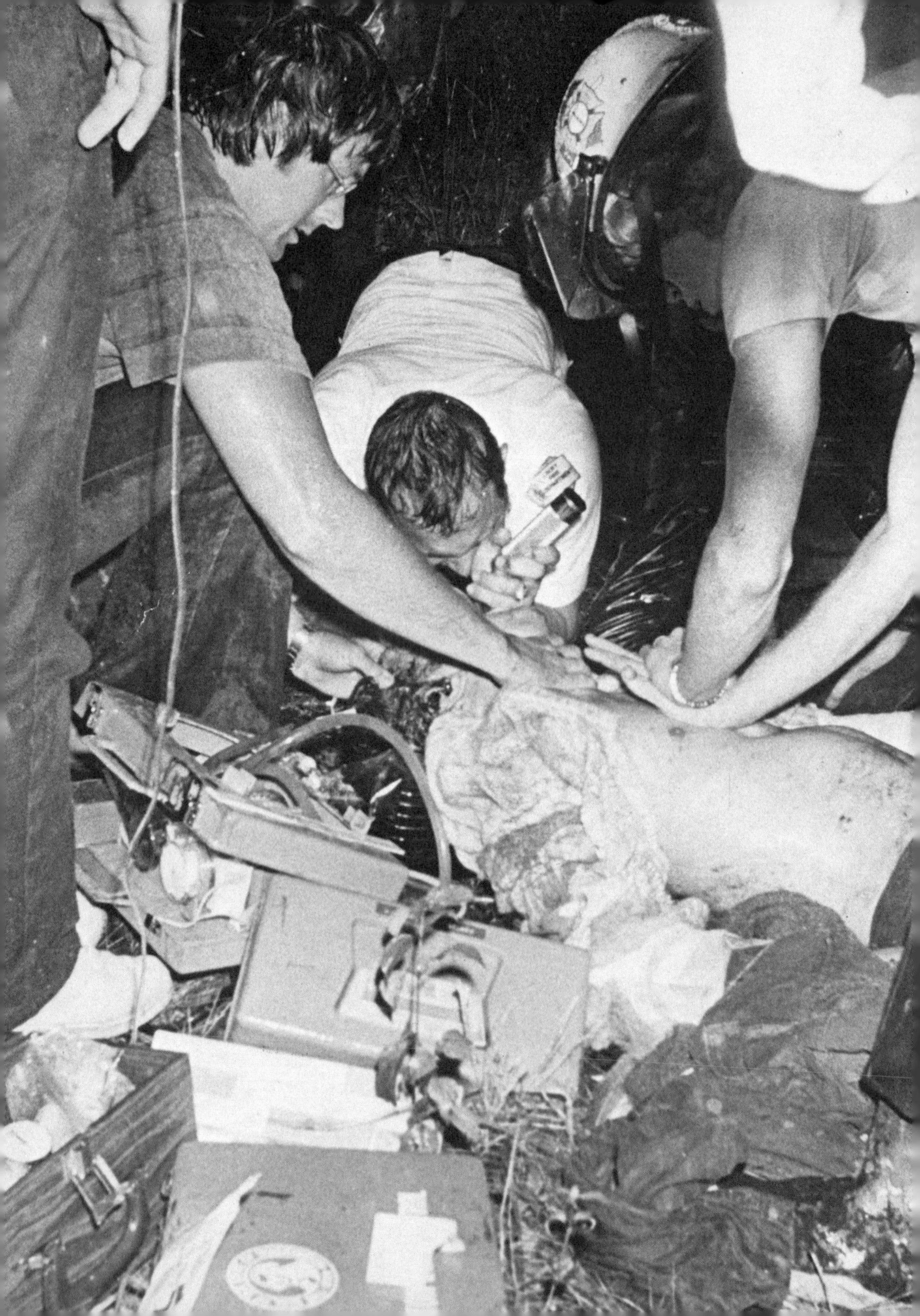

vent an ambulance from being an advanced life support system.

Every type of work has its problems, but those facing paramedics can not only be difficult for the paramedics to work with, but fatal to the public. It takes truly dedicated young men and women to become paramedics, and to remain on the job.

"Burnout shows itself most noticeably in repeated tardiness, absenteeism, boredom, low morale, daydreaming, indecisiveness, memory lapses, alcohol or drug abuse, and excessive weight gain or loss," says an official of the Chicago Fire Paramedics Association.

But sometimes, a new surge of satisfaction with their work may come, for instance when a paramedic delivers another new baby.

"It helps make up for all the rest," says one paramedic. "It puts hope and joy back into our work to help bring another life into the world. There aren't many rewards to equal the look on a new mother's face when she sees her newly born son or daughter. We can put up with a lot, to see that."

In a driving rain, with little light to break the darkness of the night, paramedics fight to save a man's life. If they fail, frustration and depression will burden them.

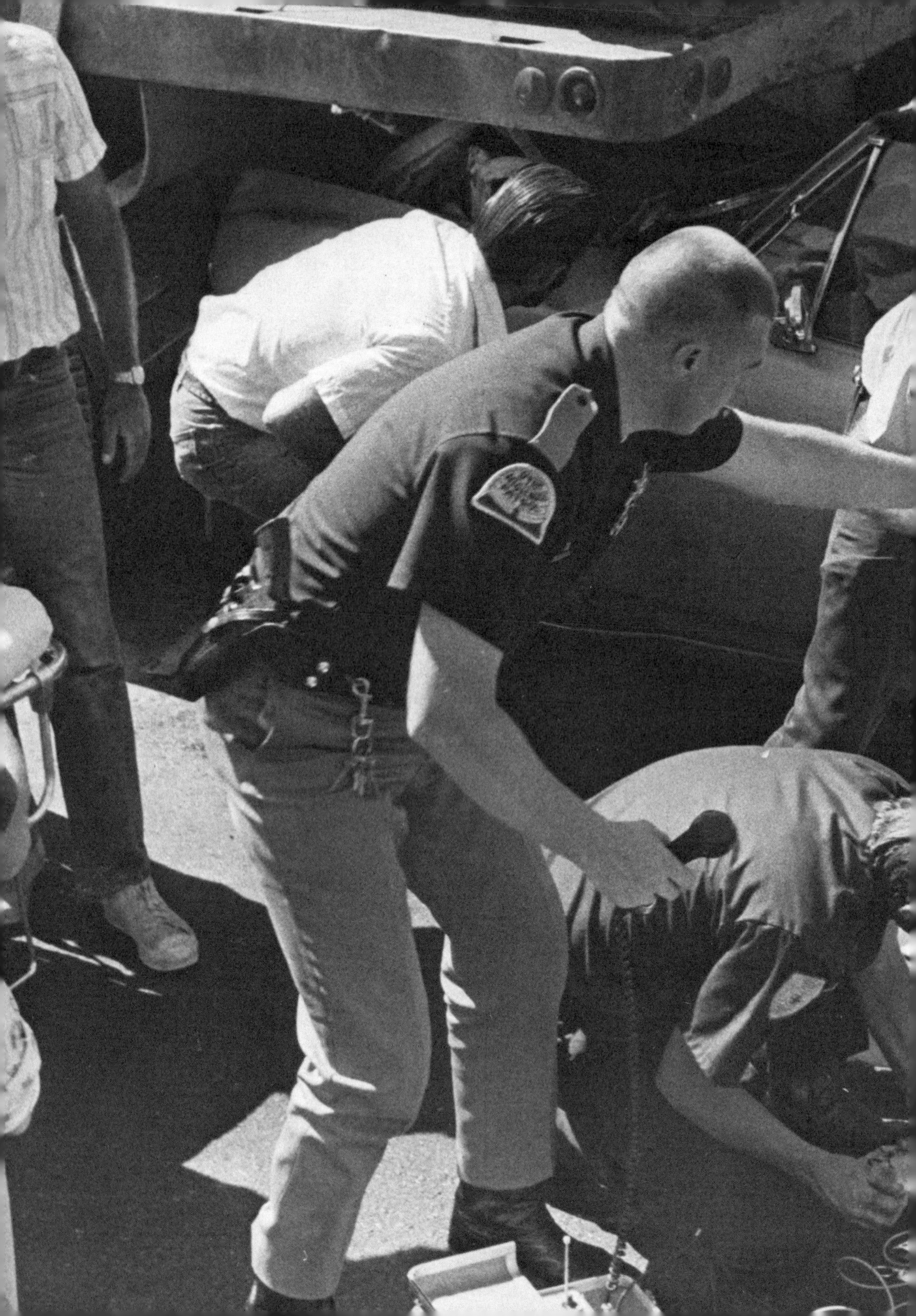

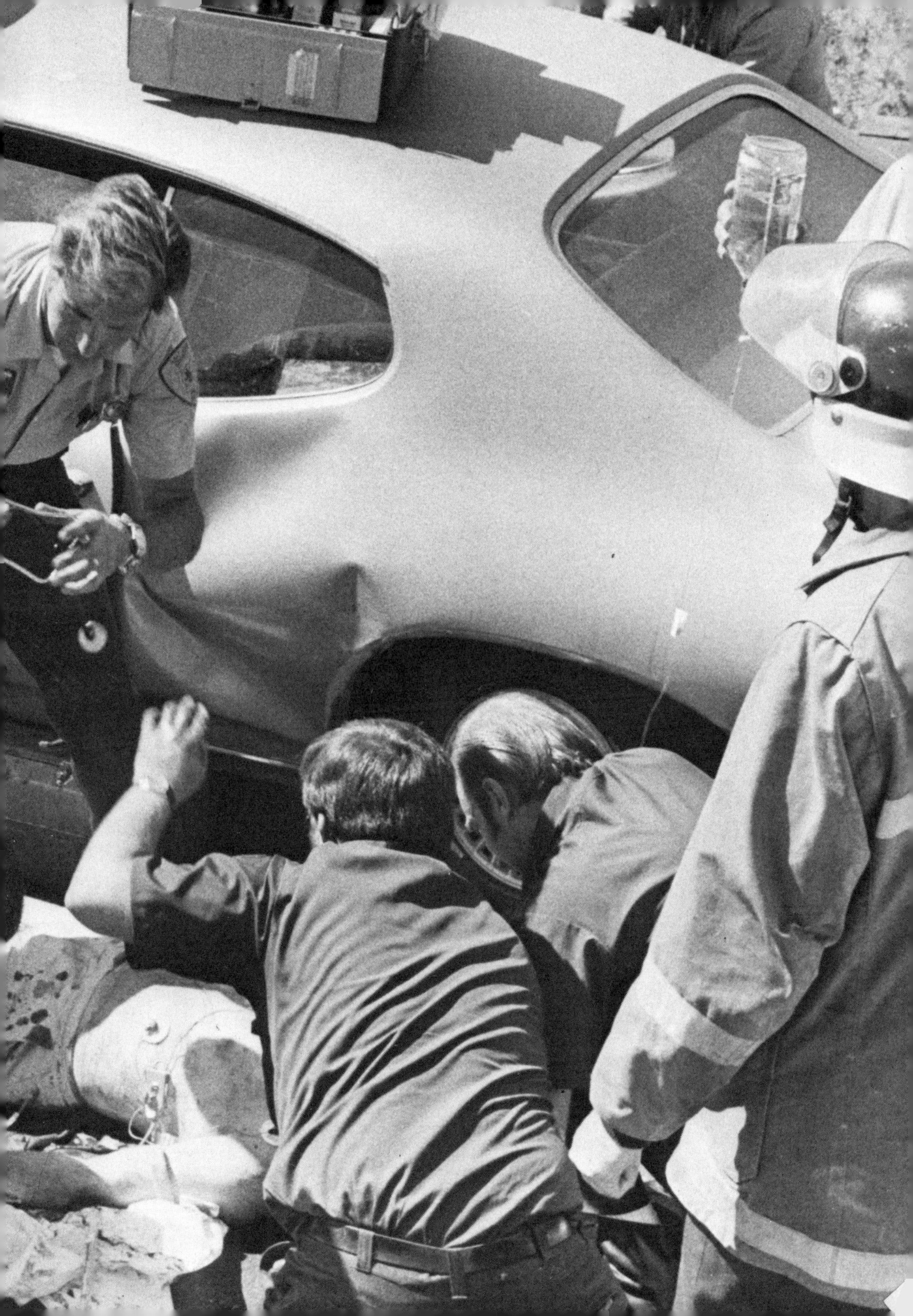

CHAPTER 8

CAREERS IN PARAMEDICS

Since paramedic and firefighting are primarily jobs for young people, it is not surprising that the minimum age for both is only 18 years in most communities. It is a wide-open field for teenagers to consider.

According to the National Association of Emergency Medical Technicians, the field of emergency medicine is growing rapidly. In some parts of the country there aren't enough young people to meet the demand.

The EMT educational requirements are set by the Department of Transportation—National Highway Traffic Safety Administration. More than 100 hours of classroom and practical study and experience, in addition to hospital observation, are required.

Requirements include instruction in management of breathing obstruction, respiratory arrest, cardiac arrest, bleeding, shock, childbirth, and environmental emergencies. Students learn how to get people

Demonstrating a new portable monitor defibrillator.

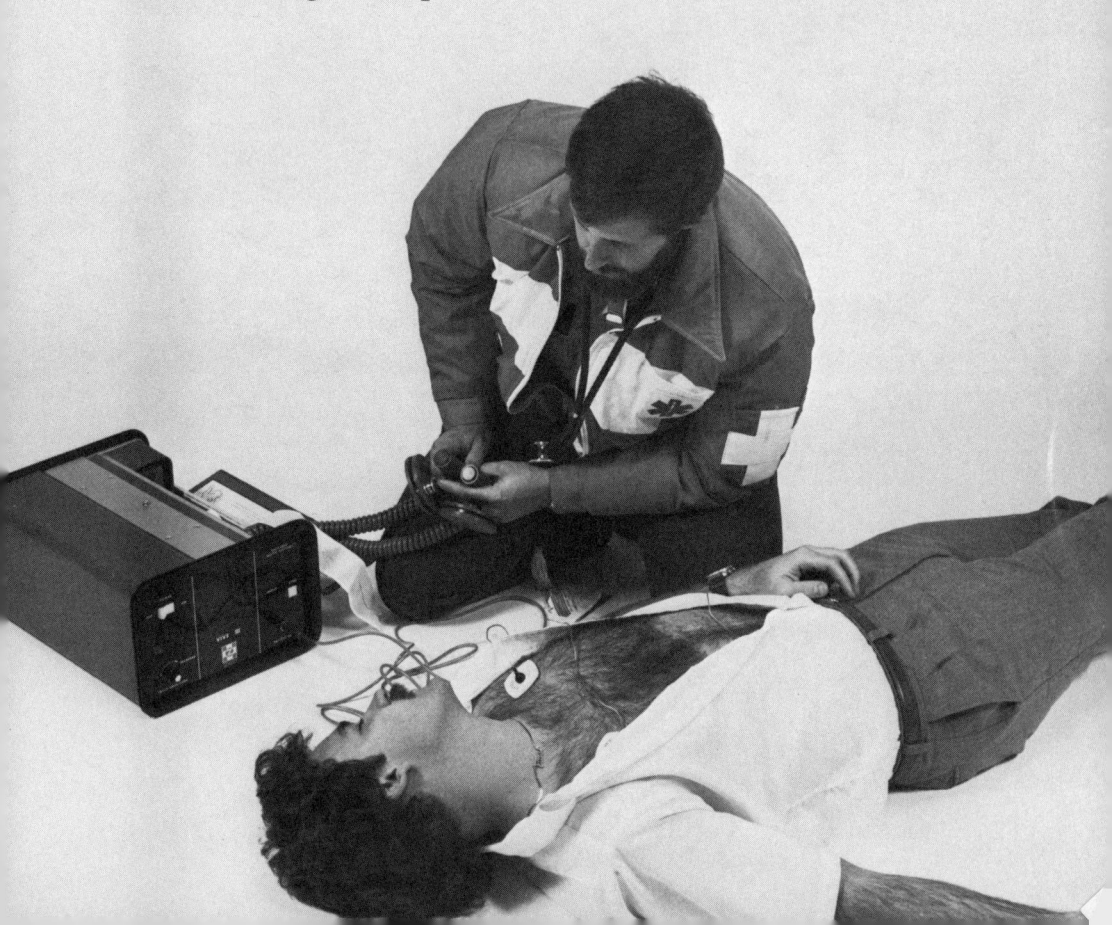

This is a demonstration of how to prepare to move a patient with probable back and skull injuries.

out of wrecked vehicles. They are also taught how to keep proper records and how to drive an ambulance. After passing the training program, EMTs usually work on a basic life support vehicle for six months before being awarded certification as an EMT-A.

The more highly trained Emergency Medical Technician-Paramedic (EMT-P) studies more advanced life support skills. Completion of the training program requires 600 to 1,000 hours of study and observation.

The EMT-P course of instruction is in three parts. The first is classroom material. The second is clinical, actually working with patients to diagnose, administer drugs, and take blood. Transfusions, cardiac monitoring, giving electric heart shocks, treating burns, helping psychiatric patients, and delivering babies are also part of clinical training. The third part of training is working under supervision as a member of the advanced life support team on an ambulance. Finally, the trainee must pass a written and a practical examination.

Life saving is serious and important work, and good training is vital.

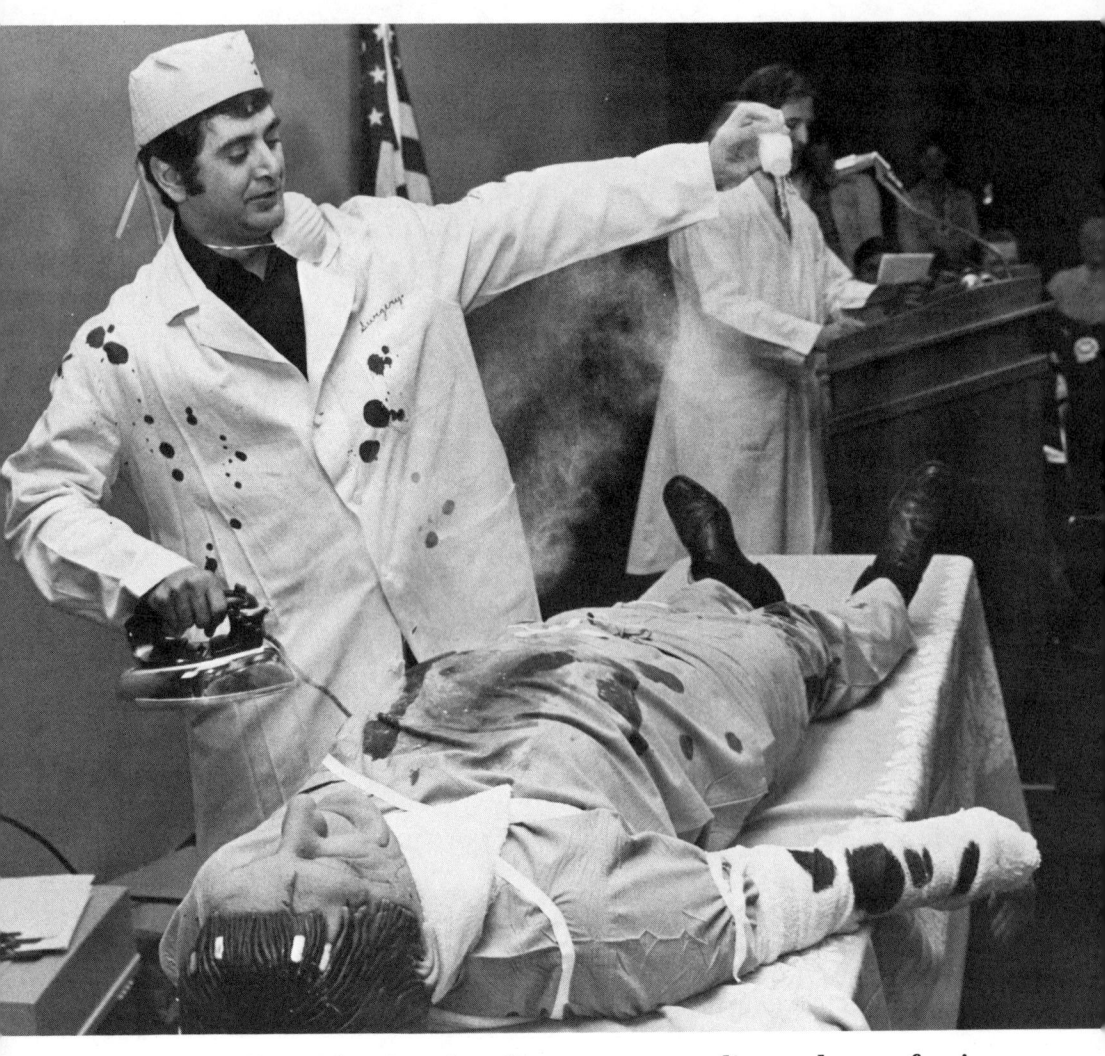

It's graduation time for new paramedics and some fun is in order after all their hard work. A humorous skit is the custom, here with a "monster" patient.

CHAPTER 9

HOW YOU CAN HELP

IN 1980, PARAMEDICS in Evanston and some other communities asked the public to help them by using something called a "Paramedic Pack." This is a small plastic container with medical information on each member of a family. The pack, given free to every household, includes a folder which explains the paramedic's job, lists paramedic emergency phone numbers, contains sheets for writing down personal medical information on each member of a family, and an identifying sticker to be placed on the right corner of the refrigerator door. The pack itself fits onto the shelf of a refrigerator with a rubber band. Paramedics look for the sticker and check the medical information in the pack before beginning treatment on any victim in the house.

The pack's medical history form describes the medical problems of family members, such as allergies, history of heart disease, high blood pressure, lung disease, diabetes, epilepsy, or if someone has a pacemaker for their heart. It also lists the name and phone number of the family's doctor and preferred hospital.

Valuable time can be saved in understanding and dealing with a patient's condition when this information is readily available to the paramedics. Check out the paramedic unit in *your* community and ask if they have a "Paramedic Pack" so you can help in time of emergency.

FOR FURTHER INFORMATION

For a list of over 350 EMT-Paramedic programs in the United States, write to the National Registry of EMTs, P. O. Box 29233, Columbus, OH 43229.

More career information can be obtained by writing the EMT/EMT-Paramedic Education Committee of the National Association of Emergency Medical Technicians, P. O. Box 334, Newton Highlands, MA 02161.

The Symbol of the Paramedic

SUGGESTED FURTHER READINGS

BOOKS:
The Paramedics, an illustrated history of paramedics in their first decade in the U.S.A., by James O. Page, Backdraft Publications, 1979, c/o *jems* magazine, P. O. Box 401, Basking Ridge, NJ 07920.

What Does a Paramedic Do?, by Kathy Pelta, Dodd, Mead & Co., 1978.

BOOKLETS:
Accidental Death and Disability: The Neglected Disease of Modern Society, Emergency Health Series A-13, 1966, Government Printing Office, Washington, DC 20401.

Course Guide, National Training Course Emergency Medical Technical-Paramedic, U. S. Department of Transportation, National Highway Traffic Safety Administration, 1977, Government Printing Office, Washington, DC 20401.

MAGAZINES:
jems, Journal of Emergency Medical Services, P. O. Box 152, Morristown, NJ 07960.

Emergency Journal, P. O. Box 159, Carlsbad, CA 92008.

Emergency Medical Services Journal, 12849 Magnolia Blvd., North Hollywood, CA 91607.

INDEX

Advanced care, 19
   life support, 24
Air National Guard, 10
Ambulance, 10, 28, 31, 43; back-up, 43; calls, 43; crews, 19, 24; technicians, 19
Automobile injuries, 10

Bandages, 19
Belfast, Ireland, 13
Bleeding, 34
Blood pressure, 10, 19
Boaters, 28
Boats, 28
Bones broken, 19, 34
Boy Scouts, 25
Breathing, 10
Burbank, California, 30
Burn care, 10, 34
Burn unit, hospital, 10
Burnout, 46, 49
Burns, Capt. Phil, 28

California, 30
Cardiac arrest, 28
Cardiac rescue technicians, 17

Cardio-pulmonary resuscitation, 19, 25, 34, 36, 37
Careers in paramedics, 52–55
Central dispatch center, 28
Central fire department dispatcher, 34
Chicago, 22, 28, 41, 43, 49
Chicago Fire Paramedics Assn., 49
Childbirth care, 19
Columbus, Ohio, 13
Communication, 15, 16, 28
Community medical cooperation, 27
Congress, 17
Cuts, 19

Defibrillation, 21
Department of Transportation, National Highway Traffic Safety Administration, 53
Disasters, 27
Dispatcher, fire department, 34
Doctors, 30, 36
Drowning, 29

Drug overdoses, 10

Earthquake, 30
Educational requirements, paramedics, 53, 55
Electric shock heart treatment, 13
Electrocardiograms, 19
Electrocution, 26
Emergencies outside United States, 30
Emergency medical technicians, (EMTs) 12, 17, 19, 22, 24, 41–43, 55; certified, 19; EMT-A, 55; EMT-P, 55
Emergency room, 10, 36, 37
Emergency! television series, 39
EMT/EMT-Paramedic Education Committee, 59
EMT educational requirements, 53, 55
Evanston, Illinois, 10, 22, 24, 28, 29, 36, 57
  Fire Department's Mobile Intensive Care Unit, 10, 22, 27
  Hospital, 10, 36

Father of paramedics, 16
Firefighters, 19, 24, 31, 34, 46
Fire station, 31, 34, 36
Firemen-paramedics, 24
First-aid treatment, 19, 25, 34

"Flying squad," 13
France, 13

Gage, John, 39
Girl Scouts, 25
Guatemala, 30

Heart attacks, 10, 13, 26; care, 19, 21; heart massage, 19
Heartmobile, 13
Helicopter rescue, 10, 28, 29
Highway Safety Act, 17

Illinois, 10, 22
Intravenous medication, 21
Ireland, 13

Lake Michigan, 28
Life-supporting drugs, 19
Lightning, 26
Loudspeakers, 34

M.A.B.A. system, 27, 28
Major emergencies, 27
Mantooth, Randolph, 39
Medical Emergency Disaster Intensive Care Specialists, 30
"M.E.D.I.C.S. International," 30
Mobile intensive care unit, 10
Mouth-to-mouth resuscitation, 19
Mutual Aid Box Alarm System, 27–31

63

Nagel, Dr. Eugent, 15, 16
National Association of Emergency Medical Technicians, 52, 59
National Registry of EMTs, 59
New York City, 13
Nursing, 30, 46

Ohio, 13
Oxygen, 10, 37
   mask, 36

Pantridge, Dr. Frank, 13
Paramedic Pack, 57, 58
Paramedics, burnout, 24; careers, 52–55; dangers of the job, 41; educational requirements, 53, 55; first unit, 10, 13; house calls, 36; interns, 24; origins, 10, 12, 13, 16, 17; retirement, 46; tests, 24; truck, 31; working conditions, 31; women, 41
Paratroopers, 17
Physicians Trained Mobile Intensive Care Paramedics, 17
Police, 19, 36
Pulse, 10

Radio-telephone communications, 9, 10, 15, 21, 36

Respiratory therapy, 46
Russia, 13

School children, 25
Senior citizens, 25
Sewer rescue, 30
Shock, 29
Snowstorms, 26
Snowmobile, 26
Splints, 19
Sprains, 19
Squawk boxes, 34
St. Francis Hospital, 24
St. Vincent's Hospital, 13

Teenagers, 52
Tornadoes, 27
Toxic fumes, 28
Tracheotomy, 21
Treatment at the scene, 34
Tunnel rescue, 30

U.S. Coast Guard, 28, 29
U.S. Department of Transportation, 19

West Germany, 13
Windpipe, 21

LOCUST GROVE ELEM. LIBRARY

2289

DATE DUE

	NOV 12				
NOV 13 1990	MAR 7				
	21				
JAN 31 1991					
OCT 24 1991					
OCT 31					
NOV 12 1991					

HIGHSMITH # 45228